To ....

From ....

Date ....

I know the lord is always with me.

Psalm 16 : 8

I am thankful for

Date ....

Today´s Bible verse

How this applise to me

I am grateful for

Prayer Requests

Note

Date ....

Today´s Bible verse

How this applise to me

I am grateful for

Prayer Requests

Note

Date ....

Today´s Bible verse

How this applise to me

I am grateful for

Prayer Requests

Note

Date ....

Today´s Bible verse

How this applise to me

I am grateful for

Prayer Requests

Note

Date ....

Today´s Bible verse

How this applise to me

I am grateful for

Prayer Requests

Note

Date ....

Today´s Bible verse

How this applise to me

I am grateful for

Prayer Requests

Note

Date ....

Today's Bible verse

How this applise to me

I am grateful for

Prayer Requests

Note

....

....

....

Date ....

Today´s Bible verse

How this applise to me

I am grateful for

Prayer Requests

Note

....

....

....

Date ....

Today´s Bible verse

How this applise to me

I am grateful for

Prayer Requests

Note

Date ....

Today´s Bible verse

How this applise to me

I am grateful for

Prayer Requests

Note

....

....

....

Date ....

Today 's Bible verse

How this applise to me

I am grateful for

Prayer Requests

Note

Date ....

Today´s Bible verse

How this applise to me

I am grateful for

Prayer Requests

Note

Date ....

Today 's Bible verse

How this applise to me

I am grateful for

Prayer Requests

Note

Date ....

Today´s Bible verse

How this applise to me

I am grateful for

Prayer Requests

Note

Date ....

Today´s Bible verse

How this applise to me

I am grateful for

Prayer Requests

Note

Date ....

Today´s Bible verse

How this applise to me

I am grateful for

Prayer Requests

Note

Date ....

Today´s Bible verse

How this applise to me

I am grateful for

Prayer Requests

Note

Date ....

Today´s Bible verse

How this applise to me

I am grateful for

Prayer Requests

Note

Date ....

Today´s Bible verse

How this applise to me

I am grateful for

Prayer Requests

Note

Date ....

Today's Bible verse

How this applise to me

I am grateful for

Prayer Requests

Note

Date ....

Today´s Bible verse

How this applise to me

I am grateful for

Prayer Requests

Note

Date ....

Today´s Bible verse

How this applise to me

I am grateful for

Prayer Requests

Note

Date ....

Today 's Bible verse

How this applise to me

I am grateful for

Prayer Requests

Note

Date ....

Today´s Bible verse

How this applise to me

I am grateful for

Prayer Requests

Note

Date ....

Today's Bible verse

How this applise to me

I am grateful for

Prayer Requests

Note

Date ....

Today´s Bible verse

How this applise to me

I am grateful for

Prayer Requests

Note

Date ....

Today´s Bible verse

How this applise to me

I am grateful for

Prayer Requests

Note

Date ....

Today's Bible verse

How this applise to me

I am grateful for

Prayer Requests

Note

Date ....

Today´s Bible verse

How this applise to me

I am grateful for

Prayer Requests

Note

Date ....

Today's Bible verse

How this applise to me

I am grateful for

Prayer Requests

Note

Date ....

Today's Bible verse

How this applise to me

I am grateful for

Prayer Requests

Note

Date ....

Today's Bible verse

How this applise to me

I am grateful for

Prayer Requests

Note

Date ....

Today's Bible verse

How this applise to me

I am grateful for

Prayer Requests

Note

Date ....

Today´s Bible verse

How this applise to me

I am grateful for

Prayer Requests

Note

Date ....

Today 's Bible verse

How this applise to me

I am grateful for

Prayer Requests

Note

....

....

....

Date ....

Today 's Bible verse

How this applise to me

I am grateful for

Prayer Requests

Note

Date ....

Today´s Bible verse

How this applise to me

I am grateful for

Prayer Requests

Note

Date ....

Today´s Bible verse

How this applise to me

I am grateful for

Prayer Requests

Note

Date ....

Today´s Bible verse

How this applise to me

I am grateful for

Prayer Requests

Note

Date ....

Today´s Bible verse

How this applise to me

I am grateful for

Prayer Requests

Note

Date ....

Today's Bible verse

How this applise to me

I am grateful for

Prayer Requests

Note

Date ....

Today's Bible verse

How this applise to me

I am grateful for

Prayer Requests

Note

Date ....

Today´s Bible Verse

How this applise to me

I am grateful for

Prayer Requests

Note

Date ....

Today´s Bible verse

How this applise to me

I am grateful for

Prayer Requests

Note

Date ....

Today´s Bible verse

How this applise to me

I am grateful for

Prayer Requests

Note

Date ....

Today´s Bible verse

How this applise to me

I am grateful for

Prayer Requests

Note

Date ....

Today 's Bible verse

How this applise to me

I am grateful for

Prayer Requests

Note

Date ....

Today's Bible verse

How this applise to me

I am grateful for

Prayer Requests

Note

Date ....

Today's Bible verse

How this applise to me

I am grateful for

Prayer Requests

Note

....

....

....

Date ....

Today´s Bible verse

How this applise to me

I am grateful for

Prayer Requests

Note

Date ....

Today´s Bible verse

How this applise to me

I am grateful for

Prayer Requests

Note

Date ....

Today 's Bible verse

How this applise to me

I am grateful for

Prayer Requests

Note

Date ....

Today's Bible verse

How this applise to me

I am grateful for

Prayer Requests

Note

Date ....

Today´s Bible verse

How this applise to me

I am grateful for

Prayer Requests

Note

Date ....

Today 's Bible verse

How this applise to me

I am grateful for

Prayer Requests

Note

Date ....

Today´s Bible verse

How this applise to me

I am grateful for

Prayer Requests

Note

Date ....

Today´s Bible verse

How this applise to me

I am grateful for

Prayer Requests

Note

Date ....

Today 's Bible verse

How this applise to me

I am grateful for

Prayer Requests

Note

Date ....

Today 's Bible verse

How this applise to me

I am grateful for

Prayer Requests

Note

Date ....

Today 's Bible verse

How this applise to me

I am grateful for

Prayer Requests

Note

Date ....

Today's Bible verse

How this applise to me

I am grateful for

Prayer Requests

Note

Date ....

Today´s Bible verse

How this applise to me

I am grateful for

Prayer Requests

Note

Date ....

Today´s Bible verse

How this applise to me

I am grateful for

Prayer Requests

Note

Date ....

Today 's Bible verse

How this applise to me

I am grateful for

Prayer Requests

Note

Date ....

Today 's Bible verse

How this applise to me

I am grateful for

Prayer Requests

Note

Date ....

Today's Bible verse

How this applise to me

I am grateful for

Prayer Requests

Note

Date ....

Today's Bible verse

How this applise to me

I am grateful for

Prayer Requests

Note

Date ....

Today´s Bible verse

How this applise to me

I am grateful for

Prayer Requests

Note

Date ....

Today´s Bible verse

How this applise to me

I am grateful for

Prayer Requests

Note

Date ....

Today 's Bible verse

How this applise to me

I am grateful for

Prayer Requests

Note

Date ....

Today 's Bible verse

How this applise to me

I am grateful for

Prayer Requests

Note

Date ....

Today´s Bible verse

How this applise to me

I am grateful for

Prayer Requests

Note

Date ....

Today´s Bible verse

How this applise to me

I am grateful for

Prayer Requests

Note

Date ....

Today's Bible verse

How this applise to me

I am grateful for

Prayer Requests

Note

Date ....

Today's Bible verse

How this applise to me

I am grateful for

Prayer Requests

Note

Date ....

Today 's Bible verse

How this applise to me

I am grateful for

Prayer Requests

Note

Date ....

Today's Bible verse

How this applise to me

I am grateful for

Prayer Requests

Note

Date ....

Today´s Bible verse

How this applise to me

I am grateful for

Prayer Requests

Note

Date ....

Today's Bible verse

How this applise to me

I am grateful for

Prayer Requests

Note

Date ....

Today´s Bible verse

How this applise to me

I am grateful for

Prayer Requests

Note

Date ....

Today´s Bible verse

How this applise to me

I am grateful for

Prayer Requests

Note

Date ....

Today´s Bible verse

How this applise to me

I am grateful for

Prayer Requests

Note

Date ....

Today 's Bible verse

How this applise to me

I am grateful for

Prayer Requests

Note

Date ....

Today´s Bible verse

How this applise to me

I am grateful for

Prayer Requests

Note

Date ....

Today 's Bible verse

How this applise to me

I am grateful for

Prayer Requests

Note

Date ....

Today's Bible verse

How this applise to me

I am grateful for

Prayer Requests

Note

Date ....

Today´s Bible verse

How this applise to me

I am grateful for

Prayer Requests

Note

Date ....

Today´s Bible verse

How this applise to me

I am grateful for

Prayer Requests

Note

Date ....

Today 's Bible verse

How this applise to me

I am grateful for

Prayer Requests

Note

Date ....

Today´s Bible verse

How this applise to me

I am grateful for

Prayer Requests

Note

Date ....

Today 's Bible verse

How this applise to me

I am grateful for

Prayer Requests

Note

Date ....

Today's Bible verse

How this applise to me

I am grateful for

Prayer Requests

Note

Date ....

Today´s Bible verse

How this applise to me

I am grateful for

Prayer Requests

Note

Date ....

Today 's Bible verse

How this applise to me

I am grateful for

Prayer Requests

Note

Date ....

Today´s Bible verse

How this applise to me

I am grateful for

Prayer Requests

Note

Date ....

Today 's Bible verse

How this applise to me

I am grateful for

Prayer Requests

Note

Date ....

Today 's Bible verse

How this applise to me

I am grateful for

Prayer Requests

Note

Date ....

Today's Bible verse

How this applise to me

I am grateful for

Prayer Requests

Note

Date ....

Today´s Bible verse

How this applise to me

I am grateful for

Prayer Requests

Note

Date ....

Today´s Bible verse

How this applise to me

I am grateful for

Prayer Requests

Note

Date ....

Today´s Bible verse

How this applise to me

I am grateful for

Prayer Requests

Note

Date ....

Today's Bible verse

How this applise to me

I am grateful for

Prayer Requests

Note

....

....

....

Date ....

Today's Bible verse

How this applise to me

I am grateful for

Prayer Requests

Note

Do it with love.

Colossians 3:23

Note

Made in the USA
Monee, IL
10 November 2024

69777644R00066